Happy Birthday Katie
Love and Kisses
Paw Paw and Maw Maw

Our Little Artist   9-12-2001

Philippe Legendre

KIDS CAN DRAW

Anything

Anything

Walter Foster™

Contents

The Circus

Fairy Tales

The Ocean

The Mountains

Attention Parents and Teachers

All children can draw a circle, a square, or a triangle . . . which means that they can also learn to draw a dragon, a dolphin, a clown—anything! The KIDS CAN DRAW learning method is easy and fun. Children will learn a technique and a vocabulary of shapes that will form the basis for all kinds of drawing.

Pictures are created by combining geometric shapes to form a mass of volumes and surfaces. From this stage, children can give character to their sketches with straight, curved, or broken lines.

With just a few strokes of the pencil, a scene will appear—and with the addition of color, the picture will be a true work of art!

The KIDS CAN DRAW method offers a real apprenticeship in technique and a first look at composition, proportion, shapes, and lines. The simplicity of this method ensures that the pleasure of drawing is always the most important factor.

About Philippe Legendre

French painter, engraver, and illustrator, Philippe Legendre also runs a school of art for children aged 6–14 years. Legendre frequently spends time in schools and has developed this method of learning so that all children can discover the artist within themselves.

Helpful Tips

1. Every picture is made up of simple geometric shapes, which are illustrated at the top of each left-hand page. This is called the **Vocabulary of Shapes.** Encourage children to practice drawing each shape before starting their pictures.

2. Suggest that children use a pencil to do their sketches. This way, if they don't like a particular shape, they can just erase it and try again.

3. A dotted line indicates that the line should be erased. Have children draw the whole shape and then erase the dotted part of the line.

4. Once children finish their drawings, they can color them with crayons, colored pencils, or felt-tip markers. They may want to go over the lines with a black pencil or pen.

Now let's get started!

KIDS CAN DRAW

The Circus

A big oval face…

starts a circus clown.

Add a bow tie…

and a smile,
not a frown.

10

Clown

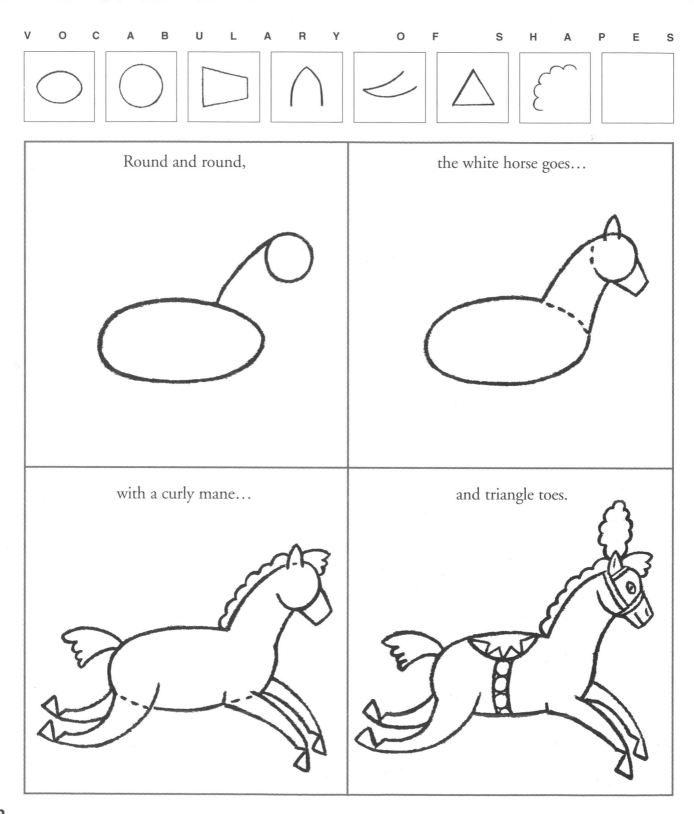

Round and round,

the white horse goes...

with a curly mane...

and triangle toes.

12

Circus **H**orse

With a big balloon body…

and a long, snakelike trunk,

he carries an umbrella…

that looks like it shrunk.

14

lephant

A square begins the trainer,

who is very brave…

to stand among the lions…

and make them all behave.

16

Lion Trainer

Straight lines make their whiskers—

the lions look like pussycats.

But when they're in the ring,

they move
like acrobats.

18

ions

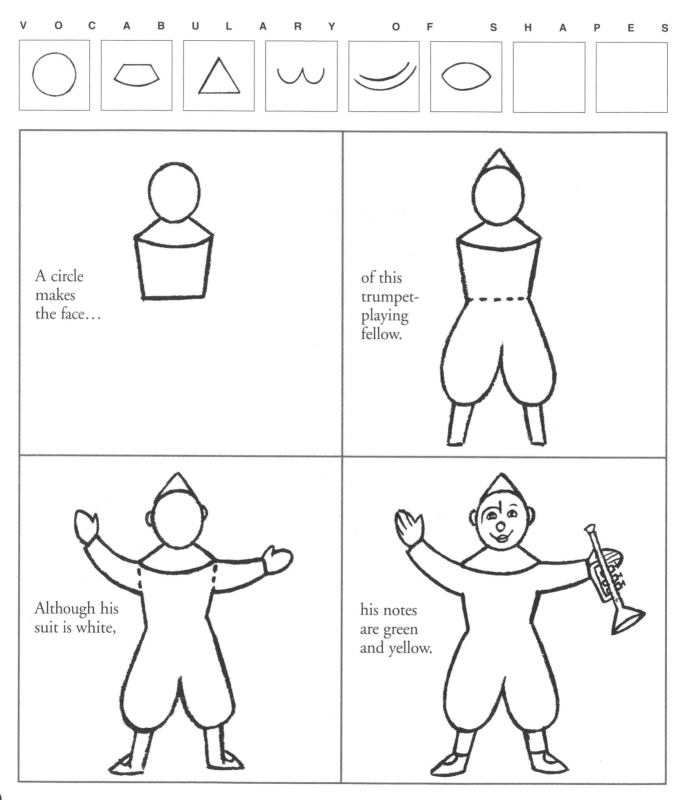

A circle makes the face…

of this trumpet-playing fellow.

Although his suit is white,

his notes are green and yellow.

Musical Clown

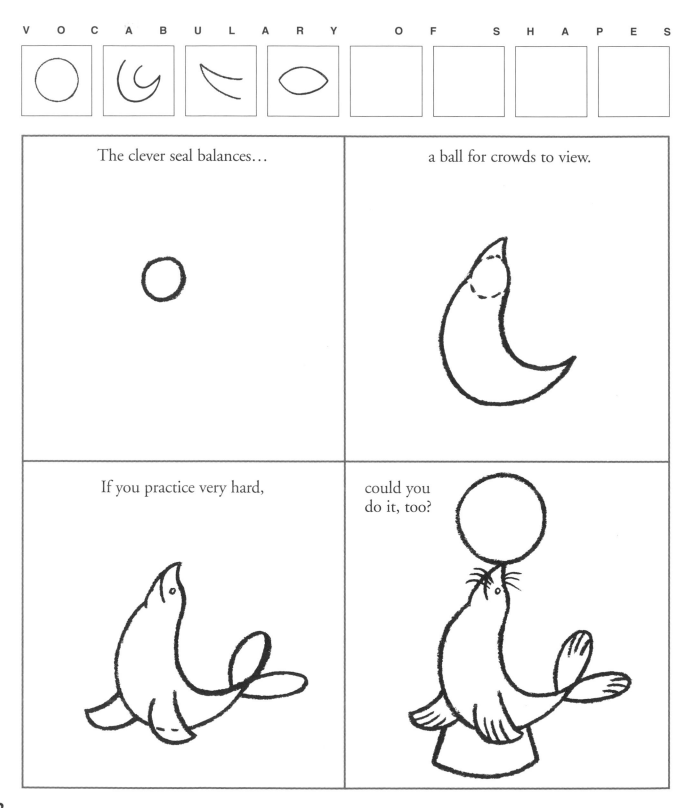

The clever seal balances...

a ball for crowds to view.

If you practice very hard,

could you
do it, too?

22

Seal

She swings from a trapeze—

watch her if you dare—

as she quickly twists and turns,

flying through the air.

24

crobat

The juggler throws the balls...

from this hand to that.

One of them is hidden...

in his little hat.

uggler

It's fun to draw a three-ring show—the circus is just dandy!

The only thing that's missing here is fluffy cotton candy.

KIDS CAN DRAW

Fairy Tales

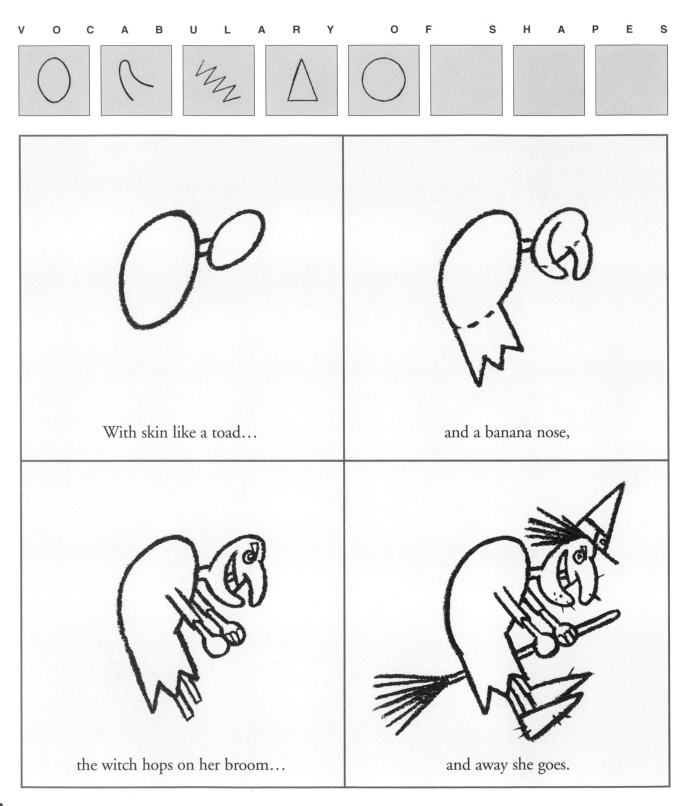

With skin like a toad…

and a banana nose,

the witch hops on her broom…

and away she goes.

32

itch

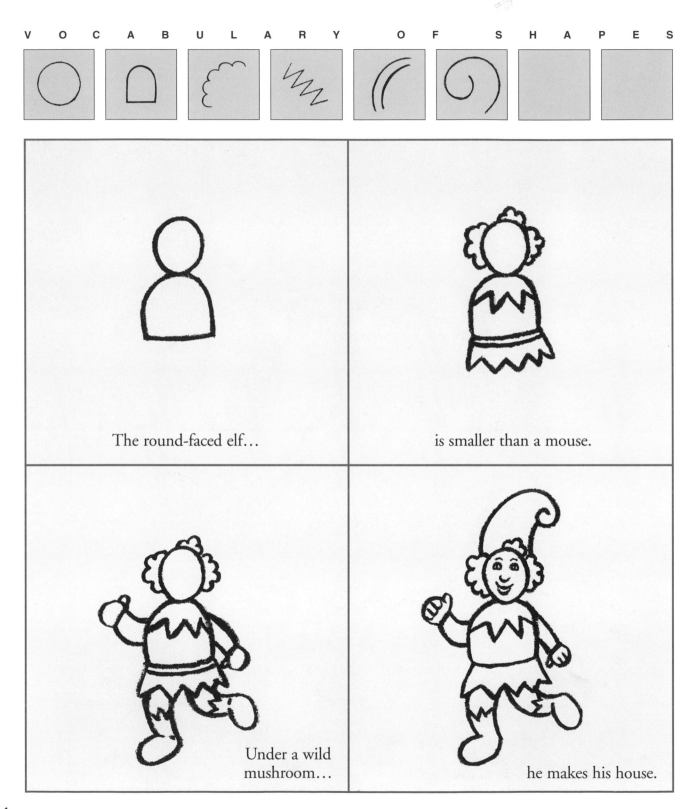

The round-faced elf…

is smaller than a mouse.

Under a wild mushroom…

he makes his house.

Elf

A sight to behold...

is the unicorn...

with her curly mane...

and golden horn.

Unicorn

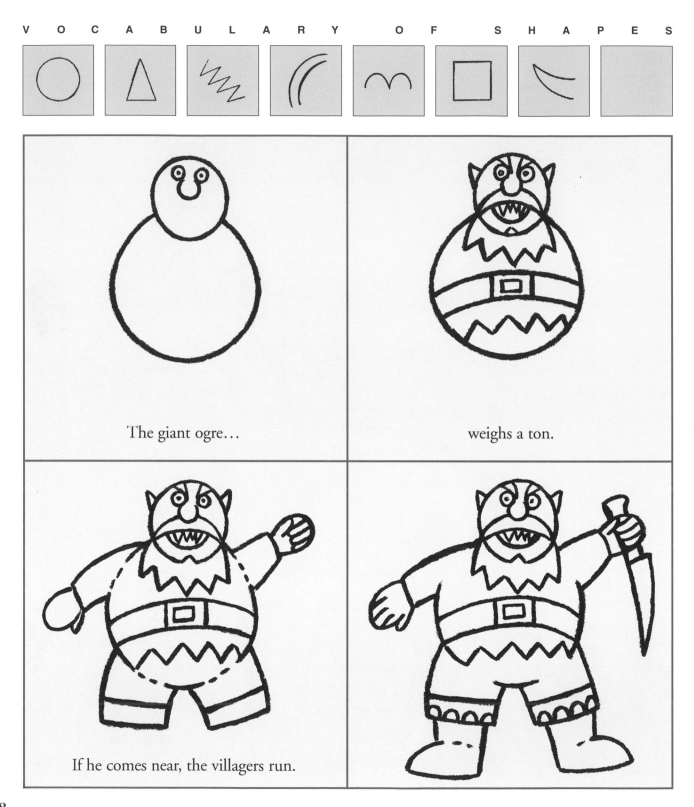

The giant ogre…

weighs a ton.

If he comes near, the villagers run.

Ogre

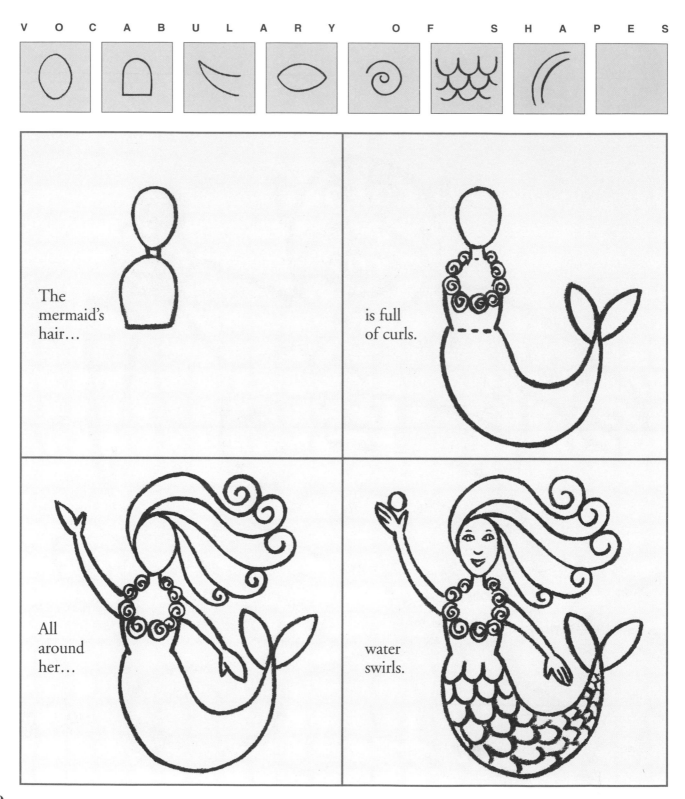

The mermaid's hair…

is full of curls.

All around her…

water swirls.

Mermaid

With umbrella wings…

the dragon flies higher,

all the while…

blowing gusts of fire.

Dragon

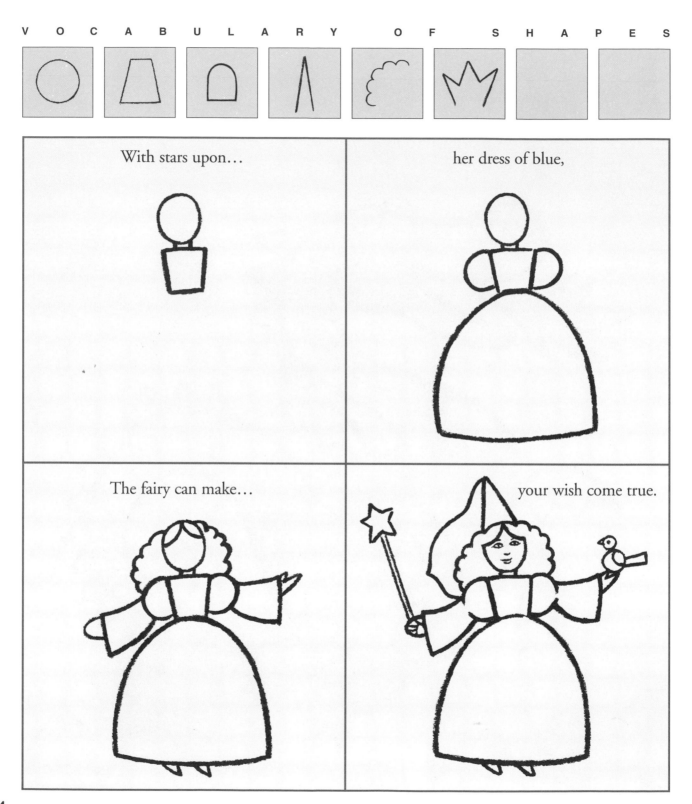

With stars upon…

her dress of blue,

The fairy can make…

your wish come true.

Fairy

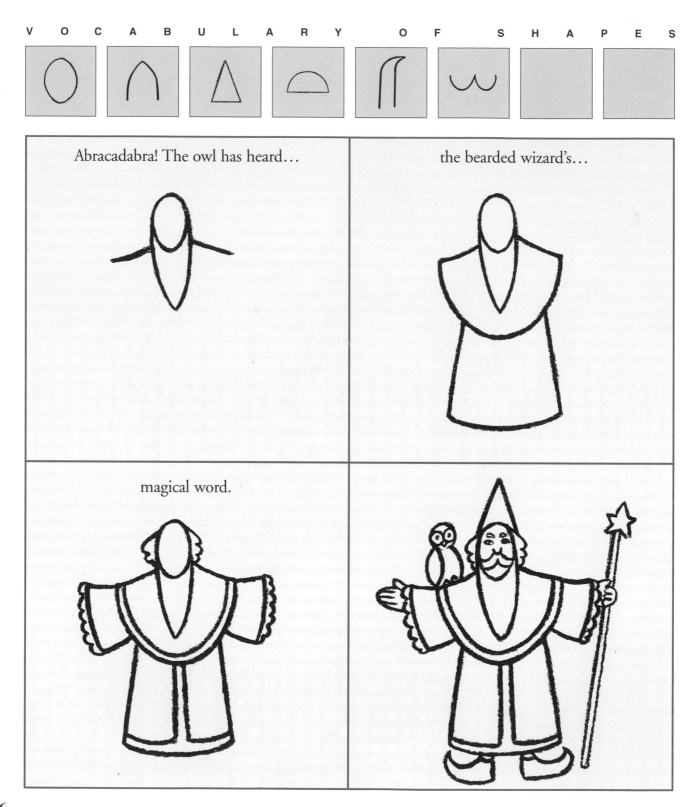

Abracadabra! The owl has heard…

the bearded wizard's…

magical word.

Wizard

With oval wings..

the pixie must…

spread her magic…

fairy dust.

48

Pixie

Although these creatures just exist in fairy tale land,

you can create them any time with a pencil in your hand.

KIDS CAN DRAW

The Ocean

With five red legs,

he's really not a fish.

Just find his star shape,

close your eyes, and make a wish.

tarfish

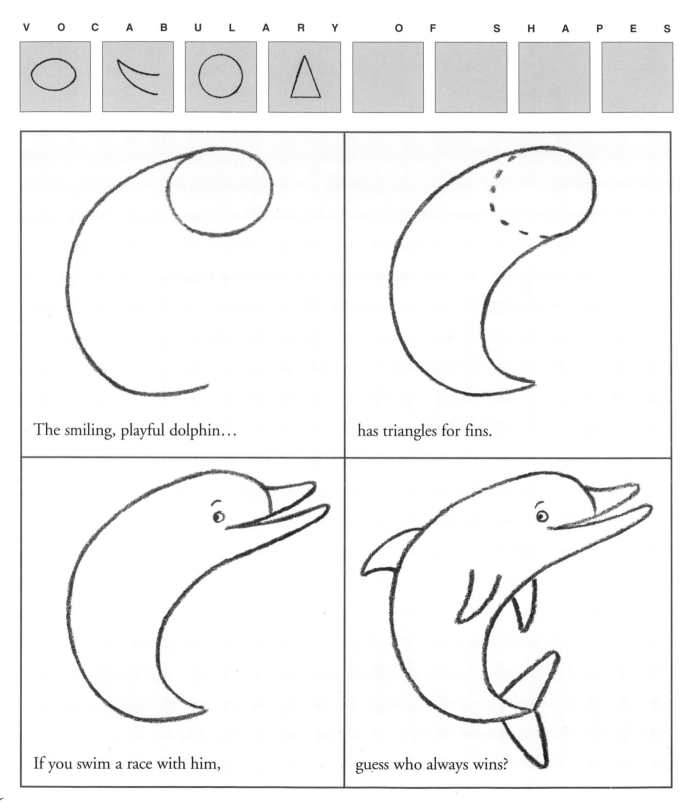

The smiling, playful dolphin…

has triangles for fins.

If you swim a race with him,

guess who always wins?

56

Dolphin

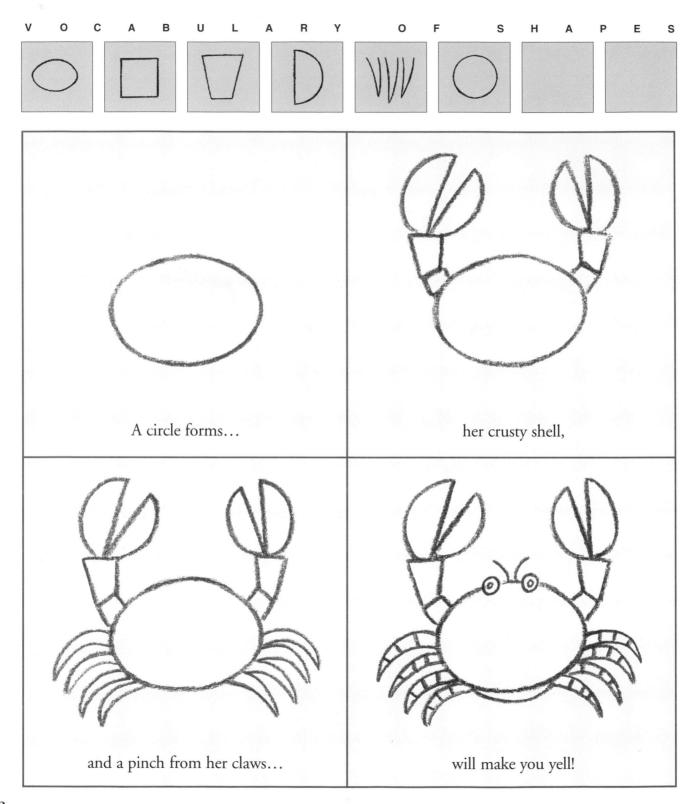

A circle forms…

her crusty shell,

and a pinch from her claws…

will make you yell!

58

Crab

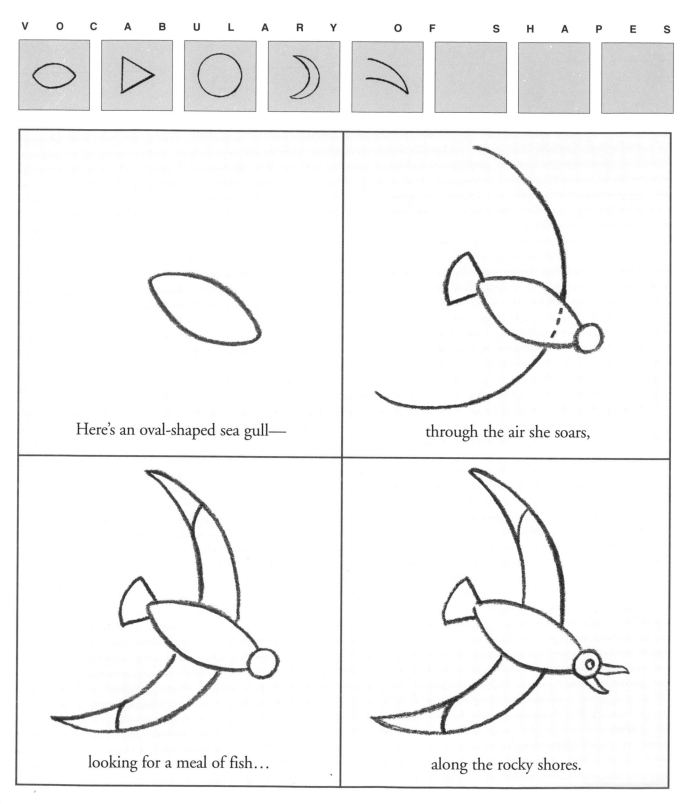

Here's an oval-shaped sea gull—

through the air she soars,

looking for a meal of fish...

along the rocky shores.

60

Sea Gull

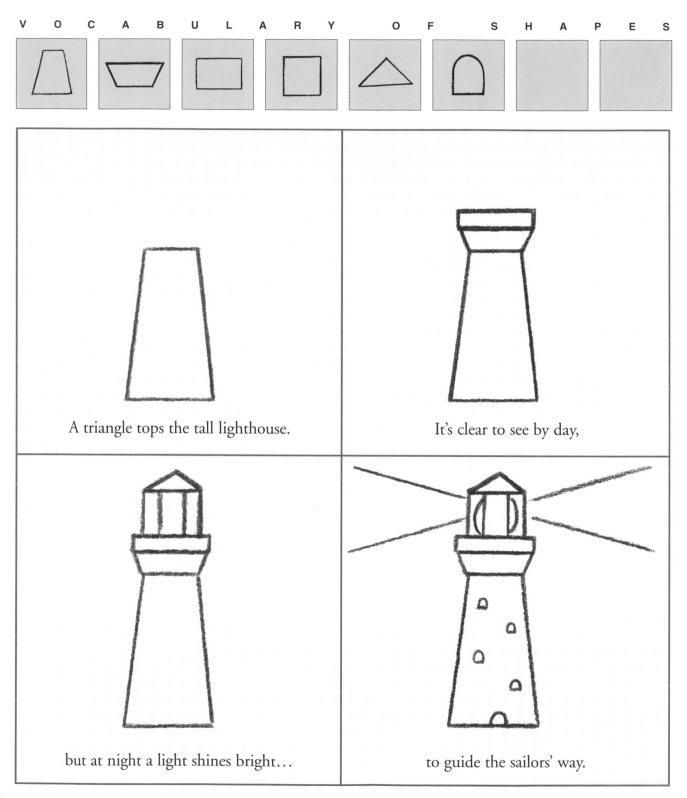

A triangle tops the tall lighthouse.

It's clear to see by day,

but at night a light shines bright...

to guide the sailors' way.

ighthouse

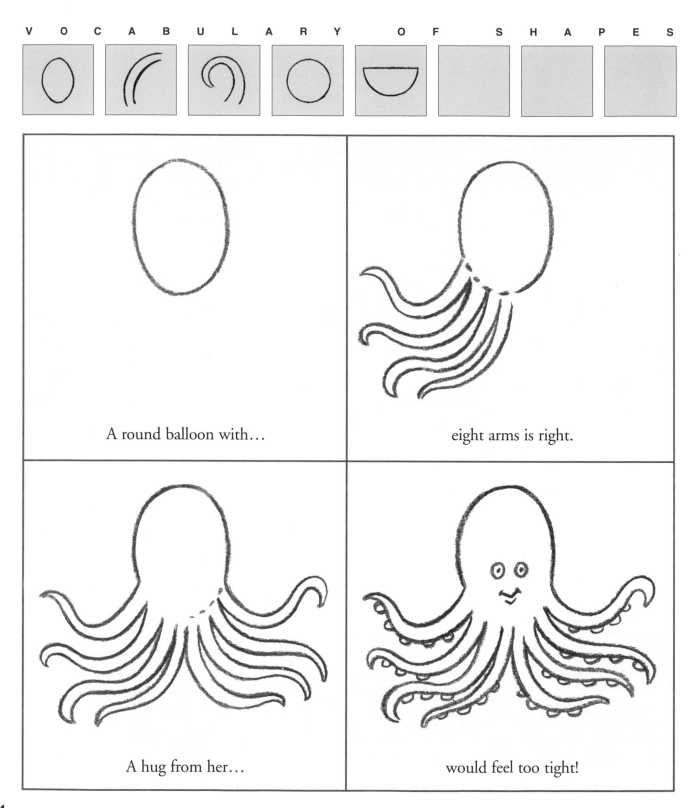

A round balloon with…

eight arms is right.

A hug from her…

would feel too tight!

ctopus

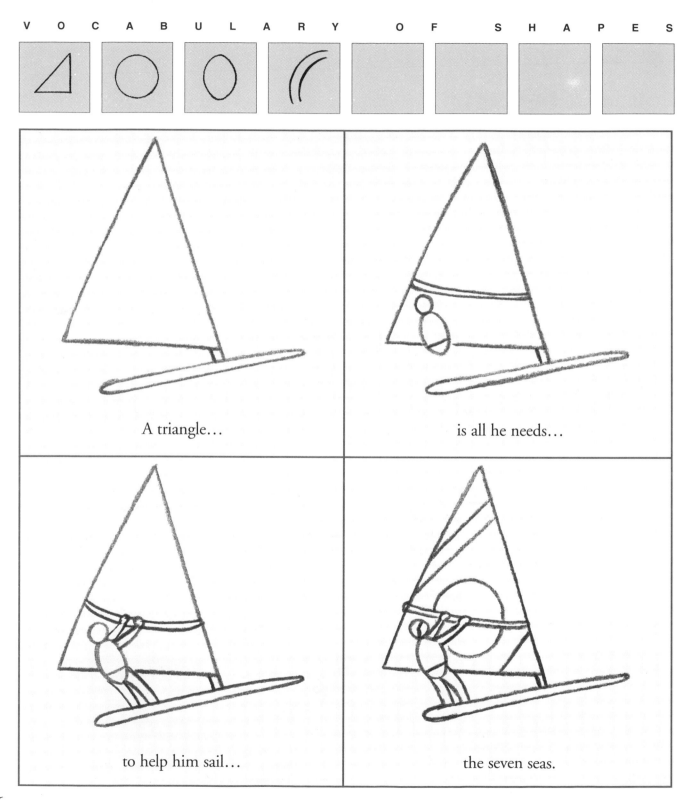

A triangle…

is all he needs…

to help him sail…

the seven seas.

indsurfer

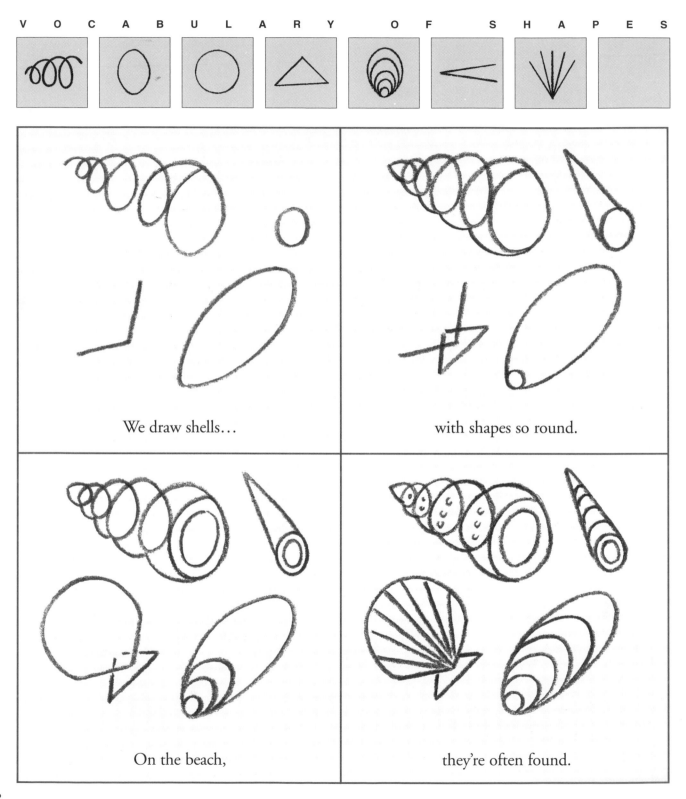

We draw shells…

with shapes so round.

On the beach,

they're often found.

Shells

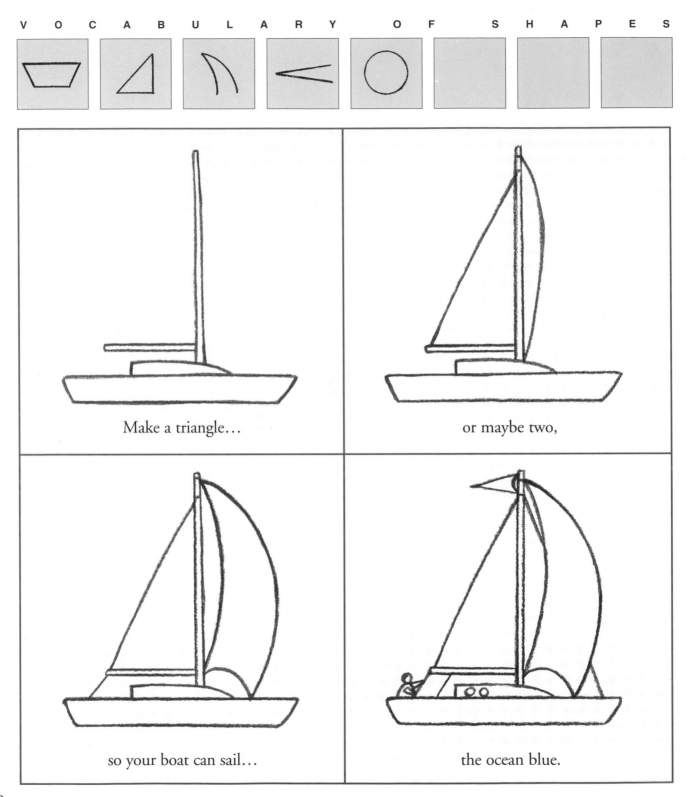

Make a triangle…

or maybe two,

so your boat can sail…

the ocean blue.

70

ailboat

Now that you have practiced and can draw them all with ease,

you can make a picture of the life around the seas.

KIDS CAN DRAW
The Mountains

In spring and fall…

and in between,

the triangle fir…

is always green.

76

Fir Tree

With two circles...

the snowman is drawn.

When the sun comes out,

he'll soon be gone.

78

Snowman

With a round, hairy body…

and a nose that's square,

this giant animal is…

a cuddly brown bear.

Brown **B**ear

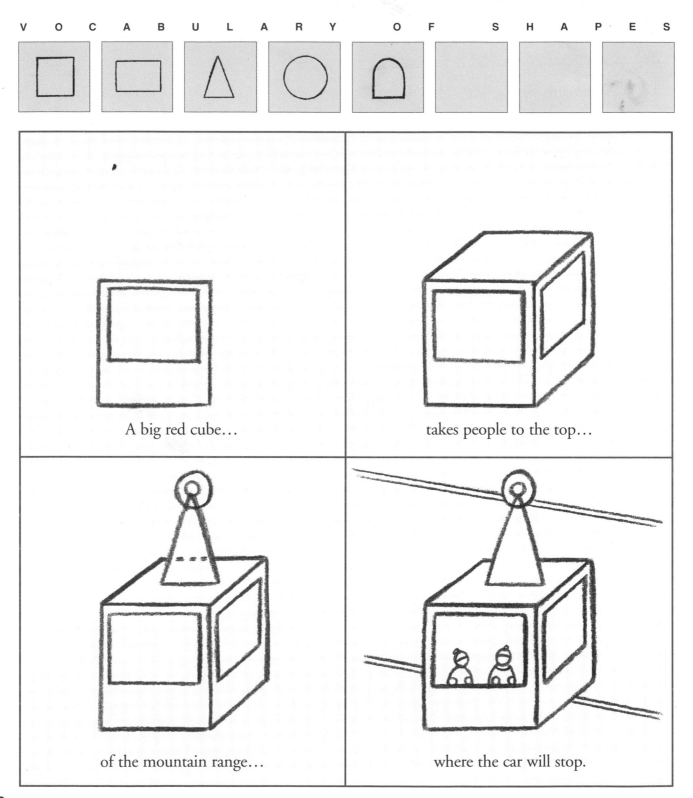

A big red cube…

takes people to the top…

of the mountain range…

where the car will stop.

82

Cable Car

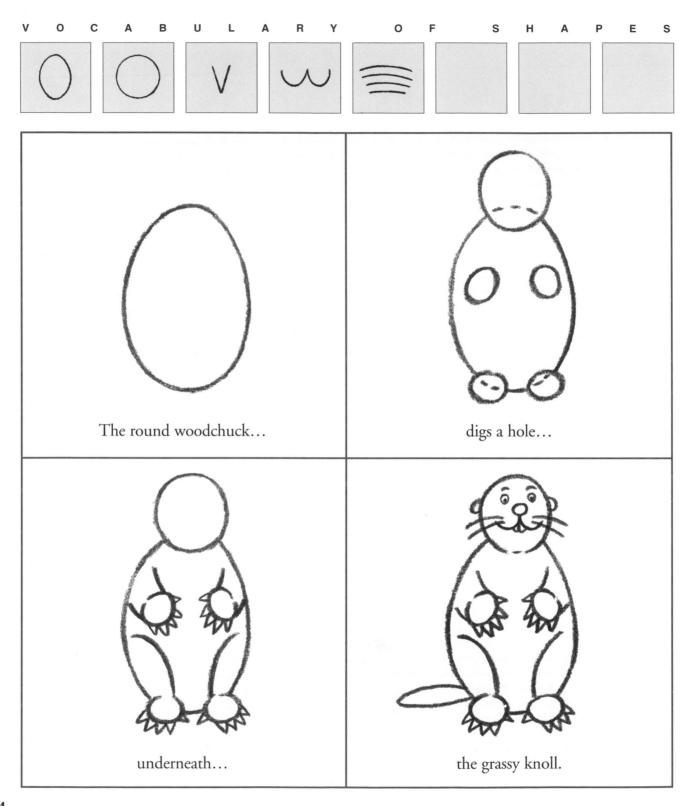

The round woodchuck…

digs a hole…

underneath…

the grassy knoll.

84

Woodchuck

The antelope…

with rounded face…

climbs the peak…

with care and grace.

ntelope

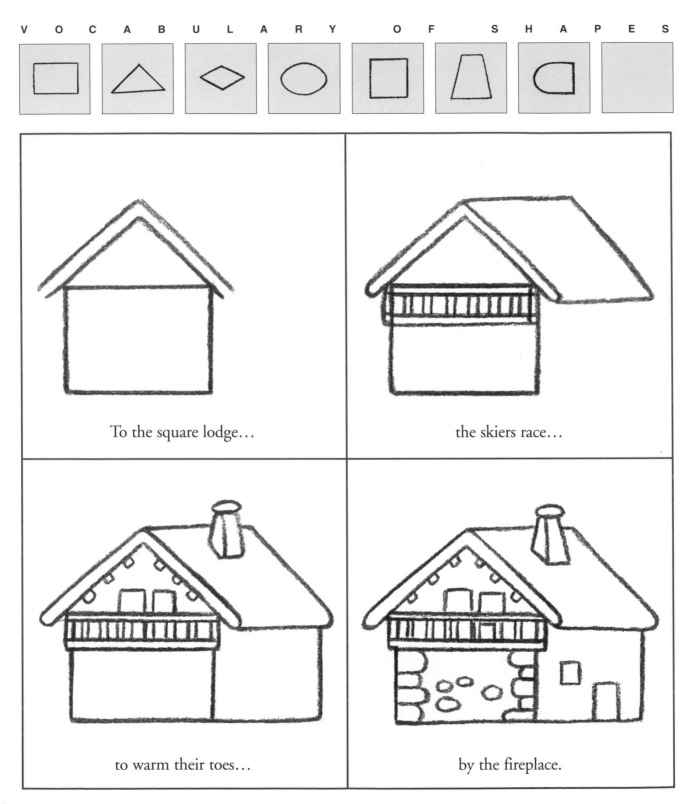

To the square lodge…

the skiers race…

to warm their toes…

by the fireplace.

Ski Lodge

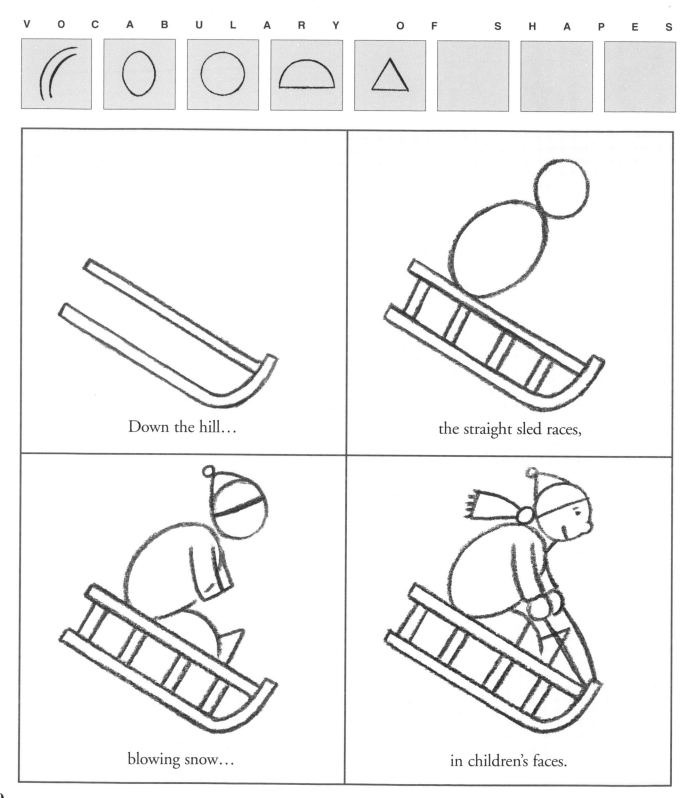

Down the hill...

the straight sled races,

blowing snow...

in children's faces.

Sled

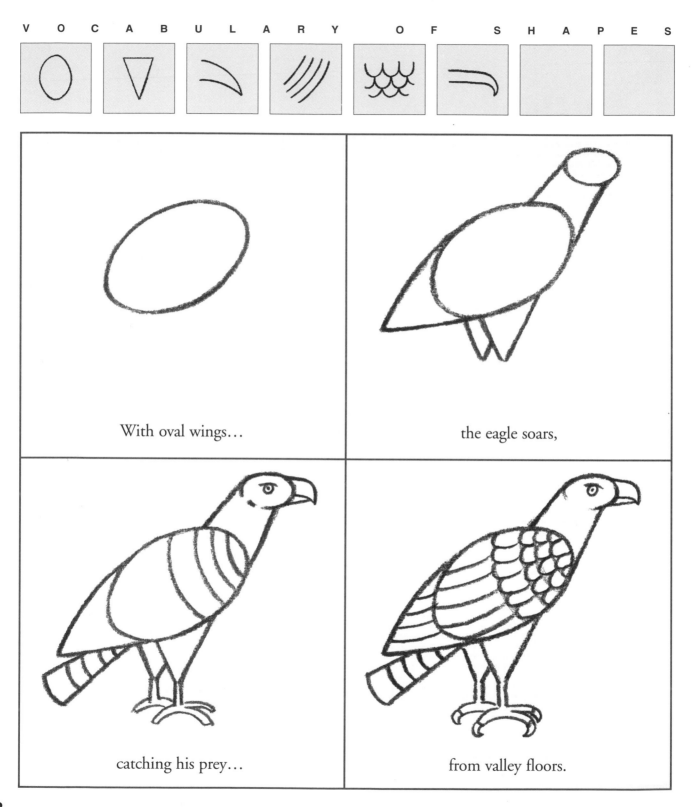

With oval wings...

the eagle soars,

catching his prey...

from valley floors.

92

Eagle

Blanketed in snowfall, it's winter in the scene.

But then springtime comes and all is green.

Walter Foster ™

Walter Foster Publishing, Inc.
23062 La Cadena Drive
Laguna Hills, CA 92653 USA
ISBN 1-56010-445-7
UPC 0-50283-33321-0